ISAAC BASHEVIS SINGER

The Life of a Storyteller

ISAAC BASHEVIS SINGER

The Life of a Storyteller

LILA PERL

Illustrated by Donna Ruff

THE JEWISH PUBLICATION SOCIETY

Philadelphia • Jerusalem   *5754 / 1994*

Manufactured in the United States of America

Library of Congress Cataloging-in-Publication Data
Perl, Lila.
Isaac Bashevis Singer : the life of a storyteller / Lila Perl ;
illustrated by Donna Ruff.
p.   cm.
Includes bibliographical references and index.
ISBN 0-8276-0512-9
1. Singer, Isaac Bashevis, 1904–1991.—Biography—Juvenile
literature.   2. Authors, Yiddish—United States—Biography—Juvenile
literature.   [1. Singer, Isaac Bashevis, 1904–1991.   2. Authors,
Yiddish.   3. Jews—Biography.]   I. Ruff, Donna, ill.   II. Title.
PJ5129.S49Z854   1994
839'.0933—dc20   93-45275
CIP
AC

10   9   8   7   6   5   4   3   2   1

Book design by Adrianne Onderdonk Dudden

Typeset by Coghill Composition Co., in Palatino and Michelangelo

*In remembrance of
my father, Oscar Perl
L. P.*

CONTENTS

ISAAC BASHEVIS SINGER

The Life of a Storyteller

1

A Little Boy on a Balcony

On a balmy afternoon in spring, Isaac, aged four, stands on the balcony of his family's second-floor apartment at Number 10 Krochmalna Street, in the Polish city of Warsaw. What a funny-sounding name for this street in the large Jewish quarter of Warsaw. *Krochmal* is the word for "starch" in both Polish and Yiddish. So Isaac really lives on "Starchy Street."

Long ago, perhaps in the Middle Ages, this old street may have been a narrow, twisting lane lined with starch sellers—people who sold the white powdery substance used for stiffening collars, cuffs, and other laundry linen. Today, though, in the year 1908, Krochmalna Street is alive with shops and with people selling *all* kinds of goods.

Isaac gazes down at peddlers offering freshly baked

*From the balcony of his family's apartment, Isaac gazes
down at the peddlers on Krochmalna Street.*

bagels. There are hawkers of salty herrings and sour pickles ladled out of deep barrels. Women from the countryside shout their wares—live chickens, fat geese, and newly laid eggs. The market stalls are heaped with sacks of grain and with dried and fresh fruits and vegetables.

For Isaac, there are wonderful little hole-in-the-wall shops where he can buy halvah, caramels, licorice, and even a chocolate-covered cookie, whenever he's lucky enough to have a few groschen to spend. Other shops located in the square at the corner of the street sell colored crayons for drawing pictures, one of Isaac's favorite pastimes.

Bargaining housewives, strollers, and loiterers throng the street beneath his balcony. Droshkies—horse-drawn wagons or carriages that double as taxis—clatter across the cobbled square. Isaac watches all of this with both delight and envy. Although all of Krochmalna Street seems to belong to him, the street is not really his to wander through or to play on. As the son of a Hasidic rabbi—a deeply orthodox and even mystical religious scholar and leader—Isaac is forced to live in a world that separates him not only from gentiles but also from many of his Jewish neighbors.

Just look at the way he is dressed on this warm spring afternoon. Instead of going bareheaded and wearing a comfortable short-sleeved shirt and knee pants, Isaac wears the round velvet cap and long satin coat considered proper for the son of a Hasid. Isaac's skin is milk-white, his eyes are a dreamy blue, while his hair is a fiery red, grown into curling, silken earlocks that dangle alongside his cheeks from beneath his velvet cap.

His hair and his clothing set him apart from the other children who know their way around Krochmalna Street or who play in the courtyard of Number 10. And this will be true even when he is seven or eight, even when he is ten and his family moves next door to a larger and newer building at Number 12 Krochmalna Street.

The courtyards attract fiddlers and acrobats, magicians and fire-eaters, who perform for money thrown down from the windows above. But these enclosed spaces are also the hangout of rowdy boys who are ready to toss clumps of mud or to poke sticks at the "Little Rabbi," whom they also call "Sissy."

There are so many things that Isaac *must* do and so many others that he *must not* do. This seems to have been true almost from the time he was an infant.

Isaac was born Icek-Hersz Zynger (or Singer) in 1904, in Leoncin, a small town outside Warsaw, located on a sandy river bank. Leoncin had been named for a generous-hearted Polish Christian landowner, Leon Christowski, who first invited Jews to settle there in 1863 after a failed Polish rebellion against the Russians. Poland had not been a self-governing country since the late 1700s, when it was divided into territories controlled by Russia, Austria-Hungary, and German Prussia. Among the many victims of the 1863 uprising were Jews who had suffered lootings and burnings that forced them out of their home villages.

By the early 1900s, when Isaac was born, Leoncin hadn't grown much. It was still a shtetl, or small Jewish town, of about forty families living in single-story houses. Isaac's father, Pinchos-Mendel, was not paid very well as the town's rabbi. Poverty, in fact, was a penalty that Pinchos-Mendel would suffer all his life for refusing to learn enough Russian to pass the official rabbinical examination. Had he done so, he would have been assigned to much better-paying posts.

In 1907, when Isaac was three, the family moved to Radzymin, yet another village outside Warsaw. Here, Pinchos-Mendel was able to earn a slightly better living as both director of the yeshiva and assistant to the chief rabbi. Here, too, Isaac began his studies at the cheder, or children's religious school. Early in life he learned that this was one of the things he *must* do.

A little over a year later, in 1908, the Singers moved once again, to Warsaw's Krochmalna Street, and Isaac's cheder studies continued. Like other children who were put to learning the Hebrew alphabet at a tender age, Isaac had to be walked to and from school through the hazardous city streets by a tutor. "School" was six days a week, from Sunday through Friday. Saturday, of course, was the Sabbath, when no writing or other forms of everyday work were done by religious Jews.

As Isaac grew a little older, he spent as many as eight hours a day in cheder, which was almost always in the teacher's house. The cheder boys sat at a long table studying the Hebrew of the Pentateuch, the first five books of the Old Testament of the Bible. As they advanced, they would undertake the reading of the laws and commentaries of the Talmud.

The teacher presided over the boys while, in the very same room, his wife might do her cooking and look after her babies. At lunchtime, she would serve the boys

Isaac began his studies at the cheder.

a soup of cabbage or potatoes with chunks of black bread. There was a little time for horseplay, teasing, and bullying among the cheder boys before they went back to the holy books and religious writings that were the life of a Hebrew scholar.

Isaac didn't exactly love going to cheder, but he didn't hate it either. He was naturally curious, and learning of any kind came easily to him. There were so many things he wanted to know. Where was God, and why couldn't God be seen? Were there really imps, demons, witches, goblins, and other terrifying creatures of the devil? Where did space and time begin, and where would they end?

The answers, though, didn't seem to lie in the holy writings he'd read so far, nor could he get them at home. Isaac's father didn't approve of all this questioning. *Faith*, he told Isaac, was the answer, *faith in the Almighty*.

At home, Isaac's life was quite different from that of his Jewish neighbors. The apartment at Number 10 Krochmalna Street contained two rooms plus a kitchen and a balcony. One of the rooms was used for sleeping. The other one served as his father's study, a small prayer house, and a rabbinical court, known as a *Beth Din*. There, Isaac's father heard and offered judgment on all sorts of religious and domestic questions.

A woman might bring in a freshly killed chicken, seeking the rabbi's assurance that it had been slaughtered properly according to Jewish law. Or she might bring him a cooking pot for meat into which a drop of milk had splashed by accident. Since the Jewish dietary rules forbade the mixing of meat and milk, could the rabbi tell her how to make the pot kosher for use once again?

Isaac's father also ruled on the problems of broken engagements, contested wills, and quarrels over inheritances. He officiated at weddings and funerals, granted religious divorces, and tried to settle lawsuits. When the parties in a dispute agreed to accept the rabbi's judgment, they silently reached out and touched his handkerchief. The case was then considered settled.

In many ways it was exciting to live in a house that was also a *Beth Din*. How many children had the chance that Isaac did to overhear squabbles and heartbreaks, to watch such an interesting variety of people enter and leave the rabbi's study? Some visitors ignored him. But others gave him a few groschen that he could spend on his beloved sweets or colored pencils. Often he was sent on errands to buy tobacco or to bring back boiled water for tea on the Sabbath, when it was forbidden to light the stove at home.

On the other hand, living in a house with a rabbinical court instead of a living room meant there were no upholstered chairs to sit on, no pictures on the walls, no ornaments or other forms of decoration. The starkly furnished room, lined with volumes of religious books, held a lectern for the rabbi, an ark—or sacred chest— for the religious scrolls known as the Torah, a long table, and several hard benches.

The apartment had only one bedroom, so it's hard to imagine where the members of the Singer family slept at night. For Isaac was not the only child. His sister Hinde Esther was thirteen years older than he, and his brother Israel Joshua was eleven years his senior. Two little sisters had been born after Israel Joshua and before Isaac. But they had died on the very same day of scarlet fever. Then, two years after Isaac's birth, his younger brother Moishe, the last of the Singer children, was born.

In his adult years, Isaac always gave his birth date as July 14, 1904. Yet, he admitted that he knew he'd been born in the Hebrew month of Heshvan. Because this second month of the Hebrew calendar falls in either October or November, his true birth date was probably some time in the autumn of 1904.

How had Isaac's birthday gotten switched to July? One of his explanations was that July 14 may have been the day in 1908 when the Singer family moved from

Radzymin to Warsaw. To comfort the baffled three-year-old—bewildered by his first train ride and his first view of bridges, trolley cars, and tall buildings—his mother offered him a special treat and told him, "Today is your birthday." The next morning Isaac discovered his balcony overlooking Krochmalna Street and, indeed, it must have seemed as though his life was just beginning.

Isaac's view of his parents came into sharp focus during the Krochmalna Street years. He began to see how different they were from each other, not only in appearance but also in background, temperament, and outlook. Isaac's mother, Bathsheba Zylberman, had grown up in the town of Bilgoray, which was a two- to three-day journey from Warsaw. It lay to the south, near the border of Austrian-occupied Poland. Bathsheba was the daughter of a distinguished rabbi who followed the Mitnaggedic rather than the Hasidic tradition. The Mitnaggedim were, in fact, anti-Hasidic, for they did not share the deep belief of the Hasidim in the unseen world of the spirits. They were more reasoned and less emotional in their approach to God and religion.

Tall, with cool gray eyes, a straight nose, a pointed chin, and brilliant red hair, Bathsheba was pursued by many suitors. She was also highly intelligent and had even taught herself to read Hebrew. A fluent knowledge of this language of the sacred texts was not considered necessary or even appropriate for women. Most Jewish women knew mainly Yiddish, the *mama loshen*, or "mother tongue," which had been derived chiefly from German and contained elements of Hebrew and of

Slavic languages as well. This tongue was in everyday use among most Eastern European Jews.

It must have been Bathsheba's deep respect for learning that made her choose the scholarly Pinchos-Mendel from among wealthier and more impressive-looking young men. In contrast to Bathsheba, he was short and round-faced. With his blue eyes, small nose and mouth, and pudgy hands, Pinchos-Mendel appeared almost womanish, except of course for his lush reddish brown beard.

In 1889, when Bathsheba was sixteen or seventeen, the two were married. As dictated by orthodox religious practice, Bathsheba shaved off her beautiful red hair and donned a fair-colored matron's wig made of goat's hair. She would wear such a wig for the rest of her life, for as her hair grew in, it was shaved regularly every few weeks.

Also, in observance of the custom known as *kest*—an extended period of boarding with the bride's family— the young couple moved into Bathsheba's father's house in Bilgoray, where they remained for eight years.

Their first two children were born in Bilgoray—Hinde Esther on March 31, 1891, and Israel Joshua on November 30, 1893. But by 1897, it had become clear that Pinchos-Mendel would never take the official rabbinical examination. He still refused to learn Russian. So the young Singers decided to take up whatever post could be found away from Bilgoray. As a result, the family made its way to Leoncin, Radzymin, and finally to Warsaw's Krochmalna Street.

The differing attitudes of Isaac's parents toward the world of the supernatural were vividly revealed in an incident that took place when Isaac was about eight years old. A poor woman arrived at the *Beth Din* on Krochmalna Street in great distress. She had spent a lot of money for a pair of geese. They had been slaughtered in the kosher manner and their heads had been removed. Yet, when she clapped the two birds together, a dreadful high-pitched wailing issued from them. The woman was fearful that the geese were inhabited by demons and that she would be cursed forever if she took them home and cooked them for the Sabbath.

Isaac's father stroked his beard gravely as three times the geese were clapped together and three times they shrieked eerily. Pinchos-Mendel, with his deep mystical beliefs, was all too ready to declare the geese possessed by evil spirits. He would have to pronounce them unclean and therefore forbidden.

But Isaac's mother, after listening each time to the chilling sound, merely laughed. True, the lungs, livers, hearts, intestines, and other internal organs of the geese had been removed. But what about their windpipes, the breathing tubes in their long necks that might still have a residue of air in them? Slapping the geese together forcefully could easily have produced that weird, whooshing sound.

As Isaac looked on in alarm, his mother calmly reached inside each goose and withdrew a bloody windpipe. Boldly, she challenged the woman to hurl the geese against each other once more and, indeed, this time they were as silent as a pair of dead geese must be. Isaac's father's Hasidic world of unseen spirits had failed to prove itself. His mother, with her rational

*Each time the woman clapped the geese
together, they shrieked eerily.*

Mitnaggedic outlook, had proved that dead geese don't "shriek."

Isaac was relieved and yet he found himself disappointed. All his life he would share some of his father's dismay at his mother's cool logic. He felt that a world of the supernatural might very well exist. Who could say no for sure?

In his adult years, Isaac often gave the example of microbes, living creatures that had been invisible until the invention of the microscope. So why *couldn't* there be imps, demons, and sprites of all sorts? What seemed unknowable today might have its existence proved beyond a doubt tomorrow, or at some other time in the future.

Although Isaac couldn't explore the mysteries of the spirit world as he would have liked to, he made several attempts to investigate more of the real world during his boyhood years in Warsaw. Sometimes he was invited to ride to the railroad station in the horse-drawn wagon of the neighborhood dairyman. Driving through the busy streets, hemmed in by droshkies, trolley cars, and the very first automobiles to appear in the city, was a heady experience for the little Hasid, who seldom ventured beyond Krochmalna Street. The train station, too, filled him with awe, and he sat anxiously in the wagon until the dairyman reappeared, carrying the heavy cans of milk he had gone to collect from an incoming freight car.

Another time, when he was older, Isaac was given a whole ruble by someone who'd sent him on an errand. A wild idea possessed him. Instead of saving the money or giving some of it to the poor, he would ride around the city in style. For an entire day he hired droshkies, bought himself sweets, and fed the swans in a park he'd never visited before. Although Polish children made fun of his Hasidic clothes and long red earlocks, he handed out candy like a generous young lord. Then, all his money spent and far from Krochmalna Street, he trudged home to the accompanying pain of a nail that had worked its way through his shoe.

On yet a more distant excursion, Isaac walked with another boy to the very outskirts of the city where there was greenery that did not exist—even in the form of a single tree—on Krochmalna Street. The two boys rambled across hills and meadows to the very banks of the Vistula, the river that flows past Warsaw to the Baltic Sea. Isaac saw men poling rafts of logs from the Polish forests to the great seaport of Danzig, where the logs would be shipped abroad for timber.

How varied and immense the world must be. Would he, Isaac, ever reach beyond the confines of Krochmalna Street? Would he ever exchange the sheltered life he led from his balcony for the kind of freedom he had tasted on his stolen country outing?

2

In Green Fields

In 1914, the year that Isaac turned ten, his family moved from Number 10 Krochmalna Street to Number 12, a newer and more modern building next door. The Singer apartment was now on the ground floor rather than one flight up, so Isaac lost his balcony and the view he had enjoyed from it. In fact, the family's quarters faced almost directly into the wall of a bakery in one of the building's several courtyards.

There were some compensations, though. Gone at last was the dim, evil-smelling staircase that had led up to the second-story apartment at Number 10. A terrified Isaac had scampered past its inky black corners for years, certain they were inhabited by imps and demons. Also, at Number 12 the apartment was lit with gaslight, which burned much brighter than the kerosene lamps

17

at Number 10. And best of all, the Singers now had an indoor toilet, a great improvement over the courtyard toilet at Number 10, which they had shared with their neighbors.

True, the rent was now twenty-seven rubles a month instead of twenty-four. Translated into dollars, the Singer rent bill went from twelve dollars a month to thirteen-fifty. This was a substantial increase for people to whom every penny counted. But Bathsheba and Pinchos-Mendel reasoned that the six-story building at Number 12, with its three courtyards, would yield many more visitors to the rabbi's court, as well as more opportunities to officiate at weddings and funerals—all means of improving the family's income.

For the first few months, things seemed to go well at Number 12. Even the bakery, which obstructed Isaac's view of the outdoors, wasn't too dreadful, for each morning it gave off the delicious smell of warm yeast and freshly baked bread and rolls. But, as the spring of 1914 warmed into summer, long-whispered rumors of a possible war were heard more and more frequently on Krochmalna Street.

The war, if it came about, would surely tear Europe apart. Already the major powers were lined up on opposing sides—England, France, and Russia against Germany and Austria-Hungary. What would happen to Poland in the event of such a war? Already part of it was in Russian hands and the rest under German and Austrian rule. Its divided territory would become a battleground, with each side seeking to enlarge its share.

Then, on June 28, an unfortunate event took place in

the far-off southern European city of Sarajevo, capital of the Austrian-held province of Bosnia. While on a royal visit, the Archduke Francis Ferdinand, heir to the Austro-Hungarian throne, was shot and killed as he drove through a street in Sarajevo. His assassin, a Bosnian, was believed to be acting for revolutionaries based in the small kingdom of Serbia, adjacent to Bosnia. A month later, Austria-Hungary declared war on Serbia. By early August of 1914, Russia, England, and France had come to the defense of Serbia and were at war with Germany and Austria-Hungary.

Almost every corner of Europe was to feel the effects of the conflict. Warsaw's Krochmalna Street was no exception. The first sign of trouble sent housewives scurrying to the market stalls to stock up on flour, buckwheat groats, dried peas and beans, and other long-lasting foodstuffs. Who knew when supplies would be cut off or how high prices would go? Of course, prices did increase rapidly because people were buying more than they needed and hoarding against future scarcity.

For the Singers, as for others, the hardships of war were soon felt in every area of family life. Isaac's grown-up sister, Hinde Esther, who had been born in 1891, had married a young man in the diamond-cutting business shortly before the war and had gone to live in Antwerp, Belgium. Now, as the German armies swept across Belgium on their way to France, her letters grew scarce and stopped coming altogether.

Isaac's older brother, Israel Joshua, was also affected by the outbreak of war. Having been born in 1893, he was now past twenty and was ordered to serve in the Russian army. The family bade him a tearful farewell as he boarded a train south to the Polish town of Tomaszow, where he was to report for duty. Days and weeks passed without a word. The family feared news of his death at the front, or perhaps at the hands of anti-Semitic Russian soldiers.

Then, late one night, he appeared at the Singer apartment, dressed in civilian clothes and carrying a false passport. Because the Germans were about to occupy Warsaw, Israel Joshua had decided to return to the city and hide out there until he would be safe from Russian seizure. The family's relief, though, was tinged with dismay. For Israel Joshua, always strongly independent in his thinking, had not only deserted the army. He also made a final break at this time with the religious life of his family. Having long expressed his opposition to Pinchos-Mendel's beliefs and practices, he now turned his back entirely on a god who could—as he put it—permit such an evil war.

Clean-shaven and wearing modern dress, Israel Joshua went to live in a Warsaw artists' studio with a group of other free-thinking young people. At first he tried his hand at drawing and painting. Then he turned to journalism and to the other forms of writing that were to become his life's work.

For the rest of the Singers, living conditions steadily worsened. The German occupation of Warsaw filled the city with refugees escaping from the areas still held by the Russians. There were few lawsuits or weddings, and Pinchos-Mendel's income dropped off sharply. During the winter of 1915, food and fuel became scarcer than

Late one night Israel Joshua appeared at the Singer apartment.

ever. Icicles formed on the window frames inside the unheated Singer apartment. Isaac would later recall breaking them off and sucking on them.

Then, in the summer of 1916, a typhus epidemic swept Warsaw. Isaac's ten-year-old brother, Moishe, came down with the high fever and red rash that were the symptoms of the disease, and the authorities took him to the hospital. Because the disease was spread by body lice, the homes of all typhus victims were required by law to be sprayed with disinfectant. The remaining family members were taken to a decontamination center, where they were kept in quarantine for eight days.

Pinchos-Mendel was so appalled at the thought of being forced to eat nonkosher food and to live in non-Jewish surroundings that he went into hiding. But twelve-year-old Isaac and his mother had to go with the police to the quarantine station. There they were stripped and bathed. Their clothing was burned, and they were given new hospital garments. Bathsheba had to give up her wig for a head scarf, and Isaac's long red earlocks were cut off for the first time since he'd grown them.

With his short hair and hospital bathrobe and trousers, he felt that he had ceased to be a Hasid or even Jewish. Worse than that, Isaac was hungry all the time. So, while his mother tried to live on nothing but dry bread, Isaac had his first taste of nonkosher food. And often he ate Bathsheba's portions in addition to his own.

In spite of the strange life he had led during his eight days at the decontamination center, Isaac resumed his religious observances after his release. And in the fol-

lowing year, 1917, he turned thirteen and became bar mitzvah, a "son of the divine law." Henceforth he would assume the religious duties and responsibilities of Jewish manhood.

There was, however, no bar mitzvah celebration, for the Singers were still suffering from hunger due to war shortages and lack of money. Even bread had become so costly that the family lived mainly on frozen potatoes, which had a sweet, rather sickening flavor. After a simple ceremony, Pinchos-Mendel gave Isaac a pair of phylacteries. The tefillin, as they were called in Hebrew, consisted of two small leather boxes—with long, narrow thongs attached—that contained writings from the Bible. Each weekday, Isaac would strap one box to his forehead and one to his left arm, in the orthodox Jewish fashion, as he recited his morning prayers.

Isaac's coming of age had taken place close to the third anniversary of the outbreak of the war. Yet all through those difficult years in Warsaw, he had never given up his dream of escaping the confines of the city for a place of green fields and open spaces. But even an afternoon's outing had become impossible once Warsaw was surrounded by troops. Then, suddenly, shortly after his thirteenth birthday, Isaac learned that his dream was about to come true. He was going for a long visit to Bilgoray, the country town in southern Poland where his mother had grown up.

It was Israel Joshua, Isaac's almost fatherly older brother, who had somehow managed to arrange things. Bilgoray, which had lain close to the border of Austrian-occupied Poland before the war, had been seized from the Russians. The entire area was now in Austrian hands, and food was said to be plentiful there. Although long lines for travel permits formed at the Austrian consulate in Warsaw, Israel Joshua shortened the process by bribing one of the German guards. Soon visas were obtained for Isaac, Moishe, and their mother to travel to Bilgoray.

Bathsheba and Pinchos-Mendel were deeply saddened at the thought of the family's separation. But they were convinced that it was necessary for the health and well-being of Isaac and Moishe. Pinchos-Mendel himself would not be going to Bilgoray. He was returning to Radzymin, the village outside Warsaw where the family had lived when Isaac was three. There Pinchos-Mendel would again become an assistant to the chief rabbi. Israel Joshua, who no longer lived with the family, would remain in Warsaw to pursue his newspaper writing.

The journey to Bilgoray left a deep impression on Isaac. It was only the second time in his life that he had ridden on a train. The first time had been in 1908, when he was not yet four years old and took a fairly short trip from Radzymin to Warsaw. But he had never forgotten the sensation. It seemed to him, as the carriage moved forward, that the cows and trees, houses and people, outside the train window, were rolling backwards.

Now, at the age of thirteen, he experienced a much longer journey through a beautifully green and fertile countryside. This new world was strangely peaceful. The train itself was almost empty. Few people had the money or the permits necessary for travel. And there was little sign of the war except for the soldiers stationed at the border, where the German- and Austrian-occupied portions of Poland met.

Beyond that point, the Singers were in the Austrian sector. There they rode a spur line built by Russian prisoner-of-war labor and finally switched to a rickety half-finished track that deposited them in Bilgoray. Altogether the journey had taken three days, with overnight stops in train stations and long waits for connections. But Isaac took in each flashing view from the train windows with fresh eagerness. Here were fruit orchards, here fields of buckwheat. Toylike villages floated past, giving way to flowered meadows and deep, dark pine forests.

At the tiny Bilgoray station, the world came alive with people once again. The entire town seemed to know that Bathsheba, daughter of the highly respected rabbi of Bilgoray, was returning home with her two young sons. There were kisses and tears, heartfelt embraces, and also the anguished news that both of Isaac's grandparents, the rabbi and his wife—whom Isaac had never known—had died since the onset of the war.

Bathsheba's older brother, Isaac's Uncle Joseph, was now the chief rabbi of Bilgoray, and Uncle Itche, her younger brother, was the assistant rabbi. Together with their wives and children, Isaac's cousins, the household overflowed. And to Isaac's surprise, he was no longer the only child in the house with bright red hair. Unlike Moishe, who was blond, there was a whole tribe of young relatives on Bathsheba's side of the family who were fair-skinned and redheaded like Isaac.

Compared with Warsaw and its dark days of hunger, Bilgoray was a land of milk and honey to Isaac. It was full summer when he arrived there. The yard was alive with running chickens. Apples and pears were ripening on the trees. Stout Aunt Yentel, Uncle Joseph's wife, filled the kitchen with the delicious scents of home-baked bread sprinkled with caraway seeds and yeast cakes laced with prune jam. There were luscious black-berries to eat, warm cookies to munch on, and plenty of fresh milk to drink.

Even so there were mumblings and grumblings among the Bilgoray grown-ups. After the death of their father, Uncles Joseph and Itche had lost some of their congregation to a local Hasidic rabbi, so money was not that plentiful. Indeed, it was good that Pinchos-Mendel had not returned to Bilgoray with his wife. Just as in Warsaw, there were more rabbis than the community could support.

Before the war, the main industry in Bilgoray had been the making of fine horsehair sieves that were exported to Russia. This work was carried on at home. The women collected and cleaned the horsehair, and the men wove it into strainers on special looms. The Austrian occupation had, of course, cut off the Bilgoray trade with Russia. Now many of the villagers worked at odd jobs for the Austrians. But who knew what might lie ahead after the war ended?

For Isaac, Bilgoray was a place to explore his innermost thoughts and to ponder his future. Wearing long ear-locks, his velvet cap, and his gaberdine coat, he once more took up his religious studies. But other kinds of reading and study had also begun to attract him.

Back in Warsaw, when Isaac was only ten, his brother

Compared with Warsaw, Bilgoray was a land of milk and honey.

Israel Joshua had given him his first nonreligious book to read. It was a copy of *Crime and Punishment* by the Russian author Dostoyevsky, translated into Yiddish. Although Isaac couldn't understand much of what he read, he was fascinated by the story about an impoverished student who kills an old woman and eventually confesses to his crime.

Novels and other worldly books were forbidden in the Singer household. Their presence led to fierce arguments between Israel Joshua and Pinchos-Mendel. Even newspapers were so unwelcome that it was only at the outbreak of the war that Isaac's father permitted the family to read them. Jewish writers, too, were outlawed by Pinchos-Mendel unless they were the authors of sacred texts.

But this had not prevented Isaac from acquainting himself with the works of the three greatest masters of Yiddish fiction of the late 1800s—Mendele Mocher Sforim, Isaac Leib Peretz, and Sholom Aleichem. Unlike the Hebrew holy books of Isaac's religious studies, these books appeared in Yiddish and consisted of stories, poems, and sketches about ordinary everyday life in Jewish villages and in the cities.

Now, in Bilgoray, Isaac further explored the humor and satire, folktales and monologues through which these Yiddish writers revealed the life that Isaac knew so well. He also began to read translations—into Polish, Yiddish, or German—of the great Russian and French novelists such as Tolstoy, Chekhov, and de Maupassant and even the American Mark Twain. He read German philosophers and difficult texts on physics and mathematics, subjects in which he'd had almost no schooling.

With the end of the war, in November 1918, even Bilgoray—which had seemed so old-fashioned and cut off from the mainstream of events—began to feel the winds of change. In Russia, in 1917, the czar had been overthrown and a communist revolution had taken place. Some young people in the town began to see communism as an answer to the world's ills. Others strengthened their faith in socialism, a milder form of economic and political change. The Zionists established a local society to promote a homeland for the Jews in Palestine. And even the traditional Jews of Bilgoray, who opposed Zionism, became newly divided on religious matters.

For the adolescent Isaac, this too was a time of restlessness and upheaval. He was examining many new ideas. Yet he still had no answers to the questions that had been plaguing him ever since his childhood in the old apartment on Krochmalna Street.

His brother Israel Joshua had been telling him for years that there *were* no answers of the kind he sought. There was only nature, cruel and uncaring, fulfilling its own needs and rhythms. But Isaac refused to believe that there was no God. Who, after all, had created nature? On the other hand, if there was a God, why was that almighty being so silent? Why did people and animals suffer? Why were there wars and butchery?

As the seasons turned in Bilgoray and Isaac grew into his middle teens, his uncertainties increased. His parents had assumed, from his early youth, that he would grow up to be a rabbi like his father, both his grandfathers, and *their* fathers. But Isaac was less and less sure about what sort of future awaited him. For he could share neither the unbelieving views of his brother Israel Joshua *nor* the blind faith of his father, Pinchos-Mendel.

a group of young Polish ruffians boarded the train. Noticing that a number of Jews occupied the car where Isaac stood, they swaggered through it calling out anti-Semitic epithets and throwing traveling bags and other belongings about. Outnumbered, the Jewish passengers tried to ignore the attack. But eventually they were forced out of their seats, which the hoodlums took over. Then, having tired of their badgering, the Polish youths leaned back and fell asleep.

Isaac arrived in Warsaw in a despondent frame of mind. Poland had once again become an independent nation at the war's end in 1918. Its people were no longer harassed by Russian, German, or Austrian occupation forces. Yet it was obvious that many Polish citizens were going to continue their long-standing harassment of one particular group among them—the Jews.

Isaac was depressed, too, about his personal life. He had resolved that he would not live with Israel Joshua and his family, for his brother had already done more than enough to help him. He planned to find lodgings in rented rooms and somehow stretch his irregularly paid salary of six dollars a week to buy himself food and other necessities.

There were both bad and good aspects to Isaac's job as a proofreader. The work, as he'd expected, was monotonous, hard on the eyes, and sometimes exasperating. The writers who contributed to *Literary Pages* often handed in material that was not quite ready to be set in print. It was Isaac's job to check through the Yiddish printers' proofs for errors and to correct them. The stories themselves, Isaac often felt, were poorly conceived and written, and he wondered why the editors bought them. Isaac harbored dreams of producing some publishable writing of his own. His head buzzed with ideas, but who would ever buy a story from him?

Though Isaac's days were now mainly full of toil and poverty, there *were* several advantages to living on his own as a young man in Warsaw. Being away from his family and having given up his religious studies, Isaac ceased to dress as a religious Jew. Gone were his earlocks and his Hasidic garments, for he now led a worldly life. As an employee of a literary journal, Isaac was admitted to the Warsaw Writers' Club, and this became for him the closest thing to a home. At the Writers' Club, one could find a warm corner in winter in which to sit and read, do some writing, or play chess. Food was sold at modest prices, and best of all, there was the society of other members of the Warsaw literary world. One could argue the issues of the day and discuss the latest articles, stories, and books that had been published.

Yiddish was the main language in which Israel Joshua and other Jewish members of the Writers' Club wrote. Hebrew, the religious and scholarly language of the holy texts and commentaries, didn't really lend itself to stories about everyday life in either the past or the present.

It was in this atmosphere of Yiddish writers that Isaac found himself translating works from German and Polish into Yiddish. He also began to write stories of his own. At first he wrote in Hebrew but soon switched to Yiddish. He hesitated, though, to show his work to anybody. Surely it was his brother Israel Joshua who

Isaac was admitted to the Warsaw Writers' Club.

was the writer in the family. It wasn't until 1927, four years after Isaac's arrival in Warsaw, that *Literary Pages* published his first work of fiction, a short story entitled "In Old Age."

Not wanting to confuse the readers of his brother's work, Isaac used the pen name Tse. About a year later, the magazine published Isaac's second story, "Women." This time he took a version of his mother's first name as his surname. He signed himself Isaac Bashevis (son of Bathsheba).

Having two stories published within a year was a modest beginning, indeed. But perhaps there *was* more than one writer in the Singer family. Isaac's father had, after all, been writing religious commentary in Hebrew all his life and, unable to find a publisher, had spent his own money to have his tracts printed. Isaac's mother, too, had done some writing. Bathsheba had secretly recorded the story of her life but later destroyed it, for it was considered improper for a religious woman to follow such a pursuit.

Saddest of all was the story of Isaac's sister Hinde Esther. In 1912 or 1913, as the young woman was traveling by train across Europe to marry a man she had never laid eyes on, she showed her mother, Bathsheba, a sheaf of stories, poems, and personal writings that she had been producing. At once, Bathsheba had ordered her daughter to tear them to bits and toss them out the train window. Her excuse was that they might be considered suspicious by the Russian guards at the border crossing out of Russian-occupied Poland.

Hinde Esther obeyed her mother, but she never truly forgave her. All her life, this eldest Singer child felt that

Hinde Esther.

she'd been ignored and belittled because she was a girl. Her parents' attention had centered on her brothers, and although she'd adored Israel Joshua, who was two years her junior, she'd been envious of his opportunities. She had never really known Isaac, for she had married and moved away while he was still a child of eight or nine.

In any case, Hinde Esther, whose marriage turned out to be deeply unhappy, continued to write using the name Hinde Esther Singer Kreitman. Before her death in London in 1954, at the age of sixty-three, she had published two novels and a collection of short stories. Her work never became well known, but scholars and literary critics who've studied it report it to be haunting and highly creative. It vividly expresses the pain and loneliness of a sensitive and talented woman who grew up in a male-dominated society.

For the next seven years in Warsaw, from 1928 to 1935, Isaac continued to do translations and to publish stories and book reviews. He also began a novel about a terrifying event that took place in a remote Polish-Jewish village, not unlike Bilgoray, during the mid-1600s. Spooky and demon filled, this story of the supernatural was titled *Satan in Goray*. It told of a young woman possessed by the devil and of the hysterical belief of the villagers in the coming of the Messiah—the long-promised deliverer of the Jews—who it turned out was a false Messiah.

Satan in Goray appeared in installments in 1934 in the Warsaw magazine *Globus*, where Isaac had become an editor. And it was published in book form in 1935 by the Warsaw Yiddish P.E.N. Club.

Although Isaac seemed to be making progress with his writing, the world around him had become darker and more troubled since his arrival in Warsaw. His life was still disorganized and unhappy. He moved from one shabby furnished room to another, never had enough money, and had been called up more than once to be examined for service in the Polish army.

Although he had so far been deferred, the prospect of being inducted into the military for a two-year term worried him constantly. He had not forgotten the episode of Jew baiting that he had witnessed on the train from Dzikow to Warsaw in 1923. Anti-Semitism had, if anything, become more open and prevalent in Poland since then, largely because of the influence of Adolf

Hitler and his Nazi followers in nearby Germany. Hitler had become chancellor (or prime minister) of Germany in 1933 and would soon gain total political control of that nation.

Isaac was troubled by other, more personal problems as well. During his years of being on his own in Warsaw, he had had several romantic entanglements. Among them was a relationship with a lively, free-thinking young woman named Runya. Although no civil or religious marriage ceremony had taken place, Isaac and Runya lived together for a time as husband and wife. And, in 1929, a son had been born to them.

Now, in 1935, the child, who had been named Israel, was nearly six years old, and Runya was urging Isaac to leave Poland and move with her and their son to the Soviet Union. Runya had long been an ardent communist. She believed that communism, as practiced in Russia since the 1917 revolution, was the answer to all the ills of society.

Isaac, however, was a long way from sharing Runya's views. He did not see communist Russia as a better place to live, *or* as a haven for the Jews. He had no faith, in fact, in any of the "isms"—not socialism or even Zionism—as a remedy for human suffering or universal injustice. Isaac did have fleeting thoughts of leaving Poland and going to Palestine to help build a homeland for the Jews. But of what use would a writer of Yiddish stories be in a place that required hardy pioneers to work the land and that, furthermore, was adopting Hebrew, not Yiddish, as its official language?

The arguments between Isaac and Runya continued. Theirs had always been a stormy relationship, and it

Runya and Isaac's son, Israel, leave for the Soviet Union.

ended, at last, when the strong-willed Runya took their young son and emigrated to the Soviet Union.

Isaac now found himself very much alone in Warsaw. His father, Pinchos-Mendel, had died in 1929, and his younger brother, Moishe, steeped in a religious life, lived with his mother in southern Poland. His older brother, Israel Joshua, was also gone from the scene. Two years earlier, in 1933, he had been invited to come to New York as a writer for *The Jewish Daily Forward*. As a result of the great tide of Jewish immigration into the United States between the 1880s and the 1920s, the *Forward* was the largest Yiddish-language newspaper in America, with a readership of about 250,000.

Israel Joshua had distinguished himself in 1932 with the publication of a novel, *Yoshe Kalb*. This title, which translates as "Yoshe the Loon," was first published in English as *The Sinner*. It was about an innocent and saintly young man who becomes the victim of power-hungry rabbinical factions, rigidity, and superstition in Austrian- and Russian-dominated Poland. The *Forward* printed *Yoshe Kalb* in Yiddish, a chapter at a time, in New York, and the story also appeared very successfully in play form on Second Avenue, the city's highly popular center of Yiddish theater on the Lower East Side.

The departure of Israel Joshua and his family for America had, however, been deeply tinged with sadness. Shortly before leaving Poland, Yasha, aged fourteen, had died of pneumonia. Grief-stricken, Genia, Israel Joshua, and their ten-year-old son Joseph did proceed with their journey in 1934, and settled in Sea Gate, an oceanside community near Brooklyn's Coney Island.

In the year that had passed since Israel Joshua had settled in America, he had grown increasingly anxious about Isaac's situation in Poland. Already there was talk of Hitler's expanding into other parts of Europe and of certain doom for Jews everywhere in his path. In Warsaw, Jewish publications were losing their readership and Yiddish writers were beginning to scatter.

For Isaac, there seemed to be no place to turn. Once again—as in the war-starved Warsaw of 1917, as in far-off Dzikow in 1923—he appeared to have reached a dead end. And once again it was Israel Joshua who opened the way for him to a new life. He managed to obtain a six-month tourist visa enabling Isaac to come to the United States.

In the spring of 1935, Isaac packed his modest belongings, consisting mainly of books and manuscripts, said farewell to his acquaintances at the Warsaw Writers' Club, and left Poland by train for Paris. After a short stay among members of the city's Yiddish literary community, he took another train for Cherbourg, on the northern coast of France. There he boarded the French steamship *Champlain* for the eight-day crossing to New York.

Never in his life had he felt so lost and so alone. Few passengers spoke Yiddish, or even Polish or Russian. Isaac knew no French or English. Only in German was he able to communicate a little. The sea stretched endlessly in all directions, and his head was filled with unanswered questions. As in his childhood, he wondered where was God and where was mercy. Why did all living creatures suffer so much misery and cruelty?

He could not help having more personal concerns as

well. Who was he—a nobody who had written a few stories and one novel in Yiddish, a language that was surely dying and was probably already dead in America? What would happen to him in the unknown and impossible-to-imagine world into which he was sailing?

4

Seeking a New Life in America

Isaac's spirits lifted some-
what on his arrival in America. He was met at the
steamship dock in New York by his brother Israel
Joshua, whom he had not seen in more than a year.
Israel Joshua, who was taller, huskier, and more strong-
featured than Isaac, appeared to Isaac to have matured
markedly.

Israel Joshua had indeed been quite successful as a
writer since arriving in New York, and he would soon
receive great acclaim for the long novel that was to be
considered his masterpiece. Titled *The Brothers Ashke-
nazi*, it was a portrayal of Jewish family life as experienced against a changing background in Poland.

Israel Joshua had brought along a writer friend of his
to meet Isaac at the ship, and now the two proceeded
to give Isaac a glimpse of the great and varied city that

would be his home. First they drove him through the streets of Manhattan, beneath clattering elevated trains and through the more elegant Fifth Avenue neighborhoods. They wound their way through the bustling Lower East Side, passing, of course, the building of *The Jewish Daily Forward*, where Israel Joshua filed his copy for his articles, stories, and serialized novels that appeared in the newspaper.

Next they crossed one of the several bridges spanning the East River from Manhattan into Brooklyn. After a fairly long drive through this large New York City borough, they arrived at its southernmost point, a stretch of beaches facing the Atlantic Ocean.

If Isaac had been dazzled by the images that had already passed before his eyes, he was even more confused by his first view of the neighborhood known as Coney Island, a combination of houses, stores, and amusement areas. Surf Avenue, Coney Island's main street, was like a perpetual carnival, lined with merry-go-rounds and sideshows, shooting galleries, and aerial tramways that formed dizzying curves against the sky. Music blared at Isaac from all sides, and the smells of sizzling frankfurters, hot sauerkraut, and greasy french fries assaulted his nostrils. Then, just as he felt his senses could bear no more, the car arrived at a police-guarded barrier at the westernmost tip of Coney Island. At a word from Israel Joshua, they passed through the barrier and into the quiet, fenced-in community of mainly private houses known as Sea Gate. This was where Israel Joshua, Genia, and their son Joseph lived.

Isaac wondered which of the scenes he had experienced in the past two hours or so was the real New York

City. In spite of a warm welcome from Genia and his twelve-year-old nephew Joseph, Isaac's head seethed and his heart was heavy once again. As in 1923, when he'd arrived in Warsaw from Dzikow, he had made up his mind that he would not live with or even take meals with Israel Joshua and his family. Above all, he would not be a burden on them.

As it turned out, rented rooms were available in Sea Gate. The community had first been developed in the 1890s as an exclusive summer resort that offered yachting and private beachfront property. But by the Depression years of the 1930s, Sea Gate had become a year-round middle-class neighborhood, and many of its imposing houses were broken up into apartments and single rooms.

Isaac settled himself in modest quarters and slowly began to explore this new world that was both fascinating and frightening to him. He took solitary walks through the quiet streets of Sea Gate and eventually left its safety to venture through the hurly-burly of Coney Island. There he discovered the Boardwalk, which ran the length of the public beach that teemed in summer with bathers seeking relief from the sweltering city.

On the Boardwalk itself were more freak shows, games of chance, and wild roller-coaster rides. Open stands sold hot dogs and a soft ice cream known as frozen custard; knishes and buttered corn on the cob; cotton candy and sweet, fizzy soft drinks such as cream soda and celery tonic. But Isaac seldom bought these snacks. Instead, he had begun eating his meals in inexpensive cafeterias.

Money was scarce. Unable to write in any language

Isaac on the boardwalk at Coney Island.

other than Yiddish, Isaac had to depend mainly on selling articles on a free-lance basis to *The Jewish Daily Forward*. Once again, he felt he was using Israel Joshua's contacts to try to earn a living, and this seemed to paralyze him when it came to writing short stories or other fiction. Even accepting a Yiddish typewriter from Israel Joshua made Isaac feel extremely guilty.

He felt ill at ease, too, about meeting other Yiddish writers at Israel Joshua's house or going with his brother to the famous Café Royal on Manhattan's Second Avenue. This was the gathering place of the city's Yiddish writers and theater people. Isaac should have felt as at home there as he had at the Warsaw Writers' Club. But instead he retreated into shyness and insecurity. He was also deeply discouraged about the future of the Yiddish language in America. The talk all around him was of the dying Yiddish theater and the dwindling number of Yiddish speakers and readers. Immigration had already been cut back sharply during the 1920s. Now, in the mid-1930s, many Jewish refugees from Nazi-dominated Germany were being denied entry into the United States.

Isaac himself was very much at risk. His six-month tourist visa had expired by the end of 1935. He *had* managed to get one extension and then another. But how long could he hope to stay in the United States without permanent papers?

As when he had lived in Warsaw, he also began to move quite often, from one shabby furnished room to another. By 1936 he was living in dreary quarters on Manhattan's East Nineteenth Street and Fourth Avenue.

Bugs crawled through the seams of the cracked lino-
leum on the floor, and he did his writing in bed rather
than on the single uncomfortable chair. Not long afterward, Isaac was back in Brooklyn, this time in the
Sheepshead Bay area, near the eastern end of Brooklyn's Atlantic Ocean beaches.

Israel Joshua, meantime, had moved to a large apartment on Manhattan's Riverside Drive. He was increasingly concerned about Isaac's chances of remaining in
the United States. Hitler had already declared that Germany must be *Judenrein*—empty of Jews. Germany's
Polish Jews were to be rounded up and shipped off to
Poland. And there was no question that, as the Germans expanded eastward, the Eastern European Jews
would be disposed of, too. Deportation to Poland was
unthinkable.

It was now 1937. The immigration laws did make it
possible for a foreigner to apply for a permanent visa
for the United States by obtaining permission to enter
the country from Canada. But there were several
catches. Isaac could not legally enter Canada as a Polish
citizen. Even *if* he managed entry, he had to have
enough money to prove to the American consul there
that he would not become a public charity case after
being admitted to the United States.

As he did so many times in the past, Israel Joshua
provided all that was needed. He paid the necessary
legal fees plus the cost of the visa. He transferred
money to Isaac's name. And he arranged for Isaac's
successful entry into Canada and back into the United
States.

Now, at last, Isaac was safe and would be able to

apply for United States citizenship (which was granted in 1943). But he was far from happy. The little boy who had wondrously watched the world from a balcony on Krochmalna Street, who had adventured happily through the green fields of Bilgoray, had long ago vanished. Isaac had grown into an uneasy youth and a guilt-ridden young man. He had learned that Runya and his son, Israel, had been stranded in Istanbul, Turkey, trying desperately to make their way from Russia to Palestine. As Isaac had predicted, the Soviet Union had proven unfriendly and even dangerous to the Jews. But he could not even send Runya money and was too ashamed to ask anyone else for help. He worried, too, about his mother and his brother Moishe, who was now a rabbi. How long would they be safe in Poland?

True, Isaac had begun selling more material to the *Forward*, but he was still not a full-time staff member. Although he was now being sent on theater-review assignments, he joked bitterly that he was always given a ticket for the second night—not the opening night, when all the "first-rate" critics were there. To him, this was a sure sign of how "second-rate" he must appear to be, compared to the real professionals in his field.

Yet he had written one novel, *Satan in Goray*, which had been published successfully in Poland. And he had not given up his dream of writing more fiction and seeing it published in the *Forward*, and even in book form, one day. Perhaps, more than anything, he needed someone in his life who believed in him deeply. That person turned out to be a woman he had met during the summer of 1937 and finally married in 1940.

She was Alma Haimann Wasserman, a German Jew who came from a family that was very different from Isaac's. Alma had grown up in Munich in a prosperous household, staffed by servants. Her father, who was well educated, was in the textile business. The Haimanns were not deeply observant Jews, and like most German Jews, they spoke German, not Yiddish, at home.

Alma had learned English as a child, had gone to school for a time in Switzerland, and had traveled to many parts of Europe. In 1927, she had married, and in 1936, she had come to the United States with her husband and two growing children to escape Hitler. There were numerous complications for Alma. She had to agree to allow her children to remain permanently in the care of their father, before she and Isaac could be married. But the two shared so many interests and she was so drawn to this strangely shy and gentle, yet strong-willed and deep-thinking man that she made the necessary sacrifices to be with him.

After they were married, the Singers moved into a modest apartment on Ocean Avenue in Brooklyn. To supplement Isaac's income, Alma immediately went to work. She was an accomplished seamstress and would eventually hold sales and executive positions in Manhattan's upscale department stores.

It was fortunate for both Alma and Isaac that they had each other at the time that the world was plunged into yet another disastrous war. On September 1, 1939, Hitler had marched his armies into Poland. Both Great Britain and France had come to Poland's defense and declared war on Germany. The "old" war, which Isaac had experienced as a boy in Warsaw and in Bilgoray, now became known as the First World War, or World War I. This new and even more terrible conflict would be called the Second World War, or World War II. Between 1939 and 1945, the year the war ended, six million European Jews—civilians, not soldiers—would die in the Nazi program of extermination known as the Holocaust. And there would be some five million other innocent victims—non-Jewish civilians from all over Europe—who would also perish at the hands of the Germans.

Isaac would later learn that his mother and his brother Moishe had died in the early years of the war, probably between August 1939 and June 1941, when the Soviet Union was an ally of Nazi Germany. The Soviets, who were then planning to share a newly divided Poland with the Germans, had deported the elderly Bathsheba and her rabbi son to a work camp somewhere in Kazakhstan, a large Soviet republic that stretched all the way from the Caspian Sea to China. There, in the middle of winter, they had been put to hard labor with the other deportees and had perished of cold, hunger, and exhaustion.

Before World War II ended, there was to be yet another death in Isaac's family. Early in 1944, at the age of fifty, his brother Israel Joshua stood foremost among the Yiddish writers of the day. Known professionally as I. J. Singer, he was producing steadily for the *Forward*. His work was also appearing in book form and in dramatized versions in the Yiddish theater, and he had recently published a new, highly praised novel. Titled

The Family Carnovsky, it was on a timely theme, for it examined the failed struggle of a Jewish family to live in Germany under Hitler, and it told of the family's experience as refugees in New York City.

Then suddenly, on February 10, 1944, Israel Joshua died of a heart attack. Although Isaac had by now become a regular staff member on the *Forward*, Israel Joshua's death plunged him so deeply into despair that he became even more paralyzed as a writer. Isaac had always thought of his brother as his "father," his "teacher," and his "master." He called his death "the greatest misfortune of my entire life."

As in Warsaw, Isaac had been signing his material with pen names so as not to confuse readers of his brother's work. One of those he had used at the *Forward* had been Isaac Warshovsky (meaning "from Warsaw").

Now that his brother was gone, could he ever presume to put forth a body of work under the Singer name, which readers so closely identified with the famous I. J. Singer? Would he, Isaac Bashevis Singer, ever emerge from beneath Israel Joshua's awesome and powerful shadow?

5

The Teller of Tales

Slowly, in the year that followed, Isaac began to recover from the shock of Israel Joshua's death and the feelings of grief and inadequacy that had engulfed him. The war ended, too, in 1945, and he knew that he must try to put behind him the haunting images of his mother's and Moishe's deaths.

Perhaps a legacy was now entrusted to him through the loss of these immediate family members. In Isaac, their past was still alive. He knew a great deal about the Jewish struggle for survival in a world that had existed for centuries and had vanished forever in the years between 1939 and 1945. That world was the one in which he'd grown up, and the memory of its ways and its people would be with him for as long as he lived. Maybe now, at last, he would be able to express himself in his writing—freely and with his own vision.

Yet the first major work to come from Isaac's pen in the mid-1940s was quite similar in form and content to Israel Joshua's work. His novel, printed in installments in the *Forward* from 1945 to 1948, even had a similar title to his brother's last book. It was called *The Family Moskat*, and it was about several generations of Polish Jews living in Warsaw from the early 1900s to the time of the Nazi onslaught.

The early 1950s saw the serialization in Yiddish of *The Manor*, another novel that was a historical saga, this time of Jewish life in Poland in the late 1800s. The 1950s also marked the beginning of a kind of short-story writing that was distinctly Isaac's and that would earn him popularity and praise through the years.

One of these early stories was called "Gimpel the Fool." It was as simple and easy to read as a folktale, and like many folktales, it seemed to contain the wisdom of the ages. The story was about a poor Jewish baker in a village in Poland who is tricked, lied to, and betrayed by everyone, including his wife. But instead of becoming enraged or trying to get even, Gimpel decides that lies are quite meaningless, for if one waits long enough, they will probably come true. And even more important, Gimpel reasons, there will be no lies in the world beyond this one.

In 1953, the American-Jewish author Saul Bellow, who himself wrote in English, happened to read "*Gimpel Tam*," as the story was titled in Yiddish, and was so impressed that he translated it into English. Shortly afterward, it was published in the literary magazine *Partisan Review*. Suddenly, Isaac's readership had grown many times its size. Who was this Isaac Bashevis Singer, where did he come from, and what else had he written?

A new world now opened up to him. Before the end of the 1950s, *Satan in Goray*, Isaac's 1930s' novel about demons and a false Messiah, had been translated into English and published in book form. "Gimpel the Fool," too, appeared between hard covers as the title story in a collection of Isaac's other short stories, all of them translated into English. At the same time, the *Forward* had begun serializing a fanciful and suspenseful new novel of Isaac's—*The Magician of Lublin*. Although written in Yiddish, it was very soon translated into English and appeared in book form in 1960.

Isaac had now been in America for twenty-five years, and although he spoke English with a Polish-Jewish accent, he could read, write, and express himself in English with great mastery. Yet he continued to write his stories and novels in Yiddish. Usually he would use an ordinary composition book with ruled pages. The only problem, Isaac complained, was the vertical line on the left side of the page. It had been put there as a margin guide for languages like English that were written from left to right. But Yiddish was written from right to left, and that line always brought Isaac up short.

Why did Isaac persist in writing in Yiddish, and how did his work get translated? Yiddish was the language in which his thoughts developed, and it was the language that best described the characters and personalities of the people in the world he wrote about. That world included more than just the Jewish towns and villages of the Polish past. It encompassed Brooklyn's

Coney Island, Florida's Miami Beach, and Manhattan's Upper West Side, where Isaac and Alma now lived.

The translation process itself was usually a collaboration between Isaac and one of the many people who acted as his translators. Isaac would do a rough translation into English, and then the two would work together on the choice of words that best carried the meaning, yet kept the spirit of the story. Much of Isaac's writing was translated by his nephew Joseph Singer, Israel Joshua's son, and some was done with the help

Sometimes Alma helped Isaac translate his work.

of Isaac's wife, Alma. Because of Joseph Singer's expert knowledge of Yiddish, he was able to compose a translation directly from Isaac's Yiddish manuscript before their collaboration.

During the 1950s, Isaac lost yet another member of his family and the last of his siblings—his sister, Hinde Esther. Although she and Isaac had never met during their adult years, after Isaac's departure for America, her death in 1954 brought back many memories. Isaac clearly recalled her frustrations and mood swings, when the family had lived together on Krochmalna Street. Some critics believe that Isaac may even have used Hinde Esther as the model for his female character in one of his most famous short stories, "Yentl the Yeshiva Boy."

Yentl is a young, unmarried woman, living in a typical Polish-Jewish village, who craves the knowledge and freedom that men enjoy. She does not want to play the limited role of a traditional wife and mother, so she cuts her hair, dons men's clothing, and sets out to be a yeshiva student in the company of the young men who frequent the study houses of the Jewish towns and villages.

In many ways, Yentl's story is a fantasy, as unlikely to have taken place as Hinde Esther's escape into the world of free expression that *she* yearned for. In any case, Isaac paid tribute to the memory of his sister on the dedication page of *The Séance and Other Stories*, one of his several short-story collections to appear in the 1960s.

Isaac "gained" a family member, too, in the 1950s.

His grown son, Israel Zamir (Zamir is Hebrew for "songbird"), came to New York from his home in the State of Israel in 1955. Isaac had not seen Israel Zamir in twenty years, since he was a child of six, and he described their meeting in "The Son," a semi-autobiographical short story that he later wrote.

In the story, the father waits at the dock in New York, anxiously searching the ship's disembarking passengers. He has only a blurred photograph with which to identify his son. There is a large, noisy crowd, and there are many highly emotional reunions. The father spies a young man who appears to be his son and calls out his name, but the new arrival is quickly claimed by somebody else.

Most of the passengers have now disembarked. Where is his son, what will he look like, and how will they communicate? His son speaks only Hebrew, and he, the father, speaks English and Yiddish. At last, the son appears, not as young or as confident as the father had expected. They greet each other awkwardly and they start a halting conversation that continues all the way home, the son speaking in modern Hebrew and the father searching for words in the Hebrew that he knows only from his religious studies.

The reunion in real life could not have been easy for either Isaac or Israel. Israel, too, wrote a memoir of their meeting, which appeared in an Israeli newspaper in Tel Aviv. But at least the gulf between the father and son had been bridged, the unhappy past could be talked about, and a more promising future relationship could start to build.

Did Isaac always write stories about people he knew

or about things that had happened to him? Often he did, but he always added some imaginative touches because, first and foremost, he believed in being a storyteller. He admitted that he drew on his childhood memories and based his characters on real people. But he also felt that the main job of fiction is to entertain. It was this blending of reality and fantasy that gave his work such an appealing quality and attracted readers curious to know—as with all good stories—*what happens next?*

It wasn't surprising, being such a magical teller of tales, that Isaac turned to writing stories for children in 1966. The only question is why he waited so long, for he was already sixty-two years old when his first children's book, *Zlateh the Goat and Other Stories*, was published.

"Zlateh the Goat," the title story, is a gentle tale that reflected Isaac's great love and concern for animals. In the story, which takes place in the countryside of Poland, times are hard for the family of twelve-year-old Aaron, so he is sent off with their goat Zlateh to sell her to a butcher in town. On the way, however, Aaron and Zlateh are caught in a fierce snowstorm. For three days, they are forced to take shelter in a haystack. There they warm each other, and Zlateh keeps Aaron alive, for she eats the hay and feeds him with her milk. When the storm subsides, the two return home together, never to part.

Wonderfully funny stories, too, appeared in the collection *Zlateh the Goat*. Isaac introduced to young readers a humorous character out of centuries-old Jewish folklore known as a shlemiel (shleh-MEEL)—a clumsy, foolish person who is always getting into all sorts of trouble. As Isaac explained in his story "The First Shlemiel," these silly, bungling folk are said to have come mainly from the Polish-Jewish village of Chelm. The shlemiel in Isaac's story is a father who is left at home to watch the baby and the rooster while his wife goes off to the marketplace. Before leaving, Mrs. Shlemiel warns her husband not to touch the pot of jam she's made, by telling him that it's poison.

But, as usual, things go all wrong for the Shlemiels. After the baby falls out of the cradle and the rooster flies away, Mr. Shlemiel becomes so depressed at the mess he's made of things that he decides to kill himself by taking poison. When Mrs. Shlemiel returns home, she discovers that her husband has eaten the whole pot of jam!

"The Mixed-Up Feet and the Silly Bridegroom" is another story that is sure to induce giggles. It opens with four sisters who sleep in the same bed. During the night they get their feet so tangled up that their mother warns them to remain in bed because they just might get up with the wrong feet. So they stay there while she goes off to Chelm, the town of shlemiels and "wise" fools, to get help. More and more silliness ensues when Yenta, the eldest daughter, becomes engaged to Lemel, who is such a shlemiel that he carries a breakable jar of chicken fat in his pocket and buries his penknife in a big pile of hay for safekeeping.

The devil and other evil characters, like the imps and goblins that terrified Isaac in his youth, also appeared in Isaac's first collection of stories for children. In "The Devil's Trick," the devil and his wife try to enter the snowbound hut where young David is alone with his baby brother. In this spine-chilling tale, with its horrifying descriptions of the threatening demons, David finally triumphs when he manages to shut the door on the devil's tail and then singes it with a burning candle.

The black-and-white drawings by artist Maurice Sendak, who illustrated *Zlateh the Goat*, were the perfect accompaniment to the stories. They evoked the loving warmth of Zlateh, the zany foolishness of the shlemiel characters, and the eeriness of the supernatural world. For his very first children's book, Isaac won a Newbery Honor Book Award. Although this was not the top prize, known as the Newbery Medal—which the American Library Association gives for the best written children's book of the year—it was the first of many increasingly important awards for literature that Isaac would receive.

Now that he was a writer of children's books as well as novels and short stories for adults, Isaac was busier than ever. Also in 1966, a collection of memoirs of his youth in Warsaw and in Bilgoray, which he had titled *In My Father's Court*, appeared in book form in English. It included, of course, many stories of life on Krochmalna Street and told about Pinchos-Mendel's *Beth Din*, or rabbinical court, as well as Isaac's family, neighbors, and boyhood adventures. Much of the material in it was so well suited to young readers that fourteen of the pieces were adapted for children and appeared, along with five newly written chapters, in an autobiography called *A Day of Pleasure: Stories of a Boy Growing Up in Warsaw*.

Unlike Isaac's purely fictional collections for children, *A Day of Pleasure*, which was published in 1969, was illustrated with photographs taken by the highly insightful pre–World War II photographer Roman Vishniac. The photos captured hauntingly the vanished world of cheder boys and Talmudic scholars, vegetable hawkers and bagel peddlers, coal porters and water carriers—all part of Jewish life in the streets and courtyards of Poland's cities before the Holocaust.

Isaac freely admitted that there was a fuzzy line between his fiction and his so-called nonfictional memoirs. Made-up material often invaded his "true" stories, and truth was usually the basis of even his wildest fantasies. But both originated in and expressed his genius as a storyteller.

What was Isaac himself like as, encouraged by success and a growing readership, he entered the sixty-fifth year of his life?

Since the early 1960s, Isaac and Alma had been living in a spacious apartment in an old-fashioned building on Manhattan's West Eighty-sixth Street, and Alma had given up her executive job at a New York department store. There was a steady stream of requests for Isaac to give lectures and interviews. There were invitations to distant places and the bestowal of numerous honors. Yet their life-style remained surprisingly simple.

In spite of almost constant interruptions, Isaac stuck as closely as he could to a daily writing schedule. Although his telephone number was listed in the Manhattan directory and his mail arrived in quantity, he had the ability to return to his manuscripts and to pick up the thread of whatever he was working on. Even while traveling by train or plane, Isaac seemed able to write. He never suffered from writer's block because of dislocation, for as he once said in an interview with the American scholar Richard Burgin, "the human ocean" was his "laboratory." From his Eastern European Jewish roots, enriched by his fascination with the "puzzle" of the human character, there flowed an endless stream of material for short stories, novels, memoirs, and children's books.

Isaac also drew much of his inspiration from the simple daily pleasures of lunching in a local cafeteria or coffee shop, strolling on Manhattan's upper Broadway near where he lived, and feeding the pigeons that flocked to the Broadway traffic islands, where elderly people sunned themselves on the benches. Even Isaac's beloved pet parakeets turned up from time to time in his writing.

He had formed the habit of eating in cafeterias back in the 1930s, when he'd lived in Sea Gate and explored the Coney Island area for inexpensive eating places. In the early 1960s, Isaac, who had always been deeply disturbed by the butchering of animals, had become a vegetarian. He was not a strict vegetarian, for he did eat eggs, an ingredient of the delicate cheese-filled crepes, known as blintzes, that he loved. Other dishes that Isaac would order in a cafeteria or a dairy restaurant were vegetarian chopped liver—made with peas, string beans, onions, and walnuts—and his favorite soup— split pea. Often his dessert was rice pudding or stewed prunes.

Isaac was so deeply opposed to killing animals for food that he had written a bloody and nightmarish

Pigeons flocked to the traffic islands on upper
Broadway, near Isaac's apartment.

short story called "The Slaughterer" about a ritual kosher slaughterer in a Polish village who so despises his work that he goes mad. Yet, in his middle and later years, Isaac no longer took himself as seriously as he had in his uncomfortable youth and young manhood. He often expressed himself with whimsy and gentle humor. On the matter of having become a vegetarian, he was once asked if he had eliminated meat and chicken from his diet because he was concerned about the health of his arteries. *No*, Isaac had replied. He had done it not for the sake of *his* arteries but for the chicken's.

On the subject of God, Isaac could also be both serious and surprisingly lighthearted. Although he had never returned to the strict observance of orthodox Judaism that he had practiced up to his late teens, he would remain a deeply spiritual person all his life. There was no question in his mind that God existed in some form, as a higher power, as nature, or in whatever other way one preferred to envision the Almighty.

At the same time, Isaac still had his boyhood complaints about God's silence, mysterious ways, and unfulfilled promises. "God," he told Richard Burgin in an interview in *The New York Times*, "must have a very good reason why He is silent. If He would begin to talk, He would have to speak in 3,000 languages and in all kinds of accents." So instead, "God speaks in deeds." But, unfortunately, ". . . we only understand a very small part of His language."

6

The Prize Years

The year 1970 heralded an era of major prize winning for Isaac. As might well have been expected, his autobiographical children's book *A Day of Pleasure: Stories of a Boy Growing Up in Warsaw* won a top honor—the National Book Award for children's literature.

At the award presentation in Boston, Isaac told the audience that there were "five hundred reasons" why he had begun writing for children. But "to save time," he would "mention only ten of them."

His reasons were really a summing up of his own philosophy of good storytelling. Isaac instinctively knew that children were the hardest readership to write for. They were easily bored by writers who were long-winded or self-involved. And they were impatient with stories written solely to send a message or deliver a moral lesson.

Like many writers, Isaac himself sometimes got carried away with too much description, prolonged rambling, or morality-tale endings. And critics sometimes pointed out such flaws in his work. But there is no question that most of the time he stuck to his credo. Here are his ten reasons for writing for children:

Number one: Children read books, not reviews. They do not give a hoot about the critics.
Number two: Children don't read to find their identity.
Number three: They don't read to free themselves of guilt, to quench the thirst for rebellion, or to get rid of alienation.
Number four: They have no use for psychology.
Number five: They detest sociology.
Number six: They don't try to understand Kafka or *Finnegans Wake*.
Number seven: They still believe in God, the family, angels, devils, witches, goblins, logic, clarity, punctuation and other such obsolete stuff.
Number eight: They love interesting stories, not commentary, guides, or footnotes.
Number nine: When a book is boring, they yawn openly, without any shame or fear of authority.
Number ten: They don't expect their beloved writer to redeem humanity. Young as they are, they know that it is not in his power. Only the adults have such childish illusions.

After receiving the National Book Award, Isaac became an ever more popular speaker to groups of children as well as adults. His lecturing took him to places as close to home as Manhattan's Ninety-second Street YMHA and as far away as the State of Israel. He received

Isaac became a popular author of children's books.

honors, almost always with Alma at his side, in Latin America and many parts of Europe. But one place to which Isaac never returned was Poland.

He knew all too well that the Warsaw of his youth would be unrecognizable. Eighty-five percent of the city had been systematically destroyed by the Germans by 1945, the end of World War II. Although the Polish government had since reconstructed Warsaw's historic center known as Old Town, its extensive Jewish sector was recalled only by the Warsaw Ghetto Monument. The city's 380,000 Jews, numbering one third of its prewar population, had been herded into the walled ghetto and starved on rations of 130 to 180 calories per day. When the Germans felt that the Jews in the ghetto were dying too slowly—only about 100,000 had perished—they began rounding them up for transport to the Nazi death camps. If not for the intervention of Israel Joshua, this might easily have been Isaac's fate.

Isaac's well-received visits to the State of Israel were, on the whole, pleasant and rewarding. His son, Israel Zamir, had married after his 1955 visit to the United States, where he had remained for two years. Now he, his wife, and their four children lived on an Israeli kibbutz, and Israel also continued his work as a journalist for a Tel Aviv newspaper.

Spending time with his grandchildren in Israel was a pleasure for Isaac, even though his halting Hebrew could not match their expert modern command of that language. But this was a minor complaint. What troubled him deeply during his stays in Israel was the lack of direct communication with his fellow Jews, few of whom among the younger generation could speak or read Yiddish. Isaac felt that in denying Yiddish as part of their people's heritage, the Israelis were failing to recognize those who had "suffered and died during the hundreds of years of exile" and without whom there would have been no Jewish state. As it was, Yiddish was dying out so rapidly all over the world that Isaac often felt like the very last holdout.

Yet he continued to write in Yiddish, even though he was sometimes responsible for so much of the English version that he credited the translation to himself. In addition to his growing output of children's and adult fiction during the 1970s, Isaac published three more memoirs that were sequels to *In My Father's Court*. Titled *A Little Boy in Search of God*, *A Young Man in Search of Love*, and *Lost in America*, they traced his difficult later years in Warsaw and his early years in America. Although these books were classified as nonfiction, Isaac freely admitted that he had changed many names, places, and dates and that he considered these memoirs to be "no more than fiction set against a background of truth." Once again, it was Isaac's free-flowing storytelling skills, superimposed on the bare facts, that made his work so fascinating.

In any case, Isaac's life in the 1970s was very different from his youthful past and even his middle years, when he'd been poor and insecure. Although still based in New York City, he and Alma now spent winters in Surfside, Florida, at the northern edge of Miami Beach, where they had purchased an apartment in 1973. In the summer they vacationed in a quiet spot in Switzerland.

As in New York, Isaac followed a surprisingly simple daily routine in Florida. He and Alma usually ate breakfast out, in a coffee shop or cafeteria. Isaac followed this with a long walk, perhaps as many as five miles. He preferred, however, to walk in Miami's shopping malls rather than on the beach, and even then he protected his fair skin and balding head with a battered cap or straw hat.

Isaac often joked about the loss of his once thick shock of bright red hair. It had started to thin while he was still in his twenties and had quickly faded in color as well to the sparse, cottony fringe that he now sported. Haircuts? Isaac hardly ever needed one. He said he took a haircut only now and then, and "*only* to keep the barber in business."

What did Isaac do on his long morning walks in Florida? Mainly he thought out his ideas for stories, developed his fantasies, and allowed impressions to come to him. So important were these walks that, when the weather was bad, Isaac would stroll instead up and down the corridor in the high-rise apartment building where he lived.

It was on the morning of a typical day in Florida, in October 1978, that Isaac went out for a short walk. Alma would be meeting him for breakfast at one of their usual haunts. But this morning she was rather late. When she finally arrived, it was with the most astonishing news. She had just been advised by telephone that Isaac Bashevis Singer had won the world's foremost literary award, the distinguished Nobel Prize for Literature!

Since his first Newbery Honor Book Award and his first National Book Award, Isaac had won several more Newbery Honors and a second National Book Award. He had been elected to many organizations celebrating literary achievement and had received honorary doctoral degrees from universities in the United States and abroad. But the Nobel Prize, which was bestowed by the Swedish foundation of that name, headquartered in Stockholm, was the greatest of them all. In addition, as a result of the bequest of the wealthy Alfred Nobel (the Swedish chemist and inventor of dynamite, who had lived from 1833 to 1896), the prize carried a cash award of $165,000.

Isaac's first reaction to Alma's news was disbelief, quickly followed by the suggestion that they should go ahead and eat breakfast anyway, since it seemed foolish to go hungry "because of happiness."

By the time they returned to their apartment, Isaac learned that his whole life was about to change. Already, reporters had descended on the building where he lived, and his phone was ringing constantly. Calls of congratulation came from United States President Jimmy Carter and from Israel's Prime Minister Menachem Begin (who, along with President Anwar el-Sadat of Egypt, had himself won the Nobel Peace Prize that year).

Although Isaac was now seventy-four years old and not in the best of health, he agreed to go to Stockholm in December for the gala award ceremonies. The months that followed the announcement were crammed with press and television interviews and requests for public appearances. Isaac and Alma had returned to New York, and for the first time in his life, Isaac had to get an unlisted telephone number. Even so, to concentrate on writing his Nobel Prize lecture, he had to flee his New York City apartment and work in a hotel-room hideaway.

In announcing the award, the Swedish Academy of the Nobel Committee had praised Isaac Bashevis Singer for "his impassioned narrative art which, with roots in Polish-Jewish cultural tradition, brings the universal human condition to life." Later, at the presentation of the award itself, Isaac would be further praised as "a consummate storyteller," a "master and magician."

Deep down, Isaac felt enormous gratification at this tribute to his work, which was also a tribute to the Yiddish language and the rich culture that it reflected. But on the surface, he continued to make his little jokes and whimsical remarks.

It was too bad, Isaac told several reporters who interviewed him, that a really great writer like Tolstoy had never received a Nobel Prize. What he, Isaac, seemed to be best at was misplacing things. He was always losing his notes, his pen, his handkerchief, his eyeglasses. *Now*, if they gave a Nobel Prize for *that*, he'd probably deserve two or three!

On the morning of December 6, 1978, Isaac and his traveling party arrived by plane in Stockholm, Sweden. The temperature in that chilly Scandinavian capital was twelve degrees Fahrenheit, but the reception Isaac received was a warm one. After being met at the airport by Swedish officials and a polite but eager battery of reporters, Isaac and Alma were driven to Stockholm's luxurious Grand Hotel. This was where most of the other Nobel Prize winners—in the fields of chemistry, physics, medicine, and economics—were hosted, and it would be Isaac and Alma's home for the days that followed. The presentation of the Nobel Peace Prize, however, took place in Oslo, Norway.

Isaac's traveling party had included two executives of his principal book publisher, Farrar, Straus and Giroux—Roger W. Straus and Robert Giroux. And *The Jewish Daily Forward*, for which Isaac had been writing since 1935, was represented by its editor, Simon Weber. A day later, Isaac's son, Israel Zamir, flew in from Israel to cover the story for his Tel Aviv newspaper. And on the day after that, December 8, Isaac delivered his Nobel lecture, which was to become part of both English and Yiddish literary history.

For the first time in its existence, the Swedish Academy was to be addressed in Yiddish. Although most of Isaac's speech was in English, his words in Yiddish—which he then translated for the audience—were perhaps the most telling. He thanked the Academy not only for the "high honor bestowed" upon him but also for its "recognition of the Yiddish language—a language of exile, without a land, without frontiers, not supported by any government."

Other points that Isaac brought up in his lecture included his firm belief in storytelling for entertainment and not for preaching. He spoke, too, of the influences of his parents and of his "brother and master," I. J. Singer, and of his personal struggle for an understanding of the ways of God. He then concluded with the assertion that "Yiddish has not yet said its last word" as the "wise and humble language of us all, the idiom of [a] frightened and hopeful humanity."

Isaac's despair about the death of Yiddish really did seem to lessen somewhat when, after the lecture, he joked, "It's a sick language. But in our people's history the difference between sick and dead is a big one."

The following day was a Saturday, and although no longer a fully observant Jew, Isaac attended Sabbath services at Stockholm's Grand Synagogue. There he was honored with an invitation to read a portion from the Torah, and he also spoke briefly to the congregation.

Sunday, December 10, was the crowning day of the entire event. It began with the award ceremony itself, attended by the king and queen of Sweden, at which Isaac in formal white tie and tails received his diploma, his gold medal, and his check for $165,000 on the stage of the Stockholm Concert Hall. A banquet and a ball in the city's elegant Town Hall followed.

At a brief after-dinner speech, Isaac, bent and birdlike but with his blue eyes twinkling, told the king of Sweden and all of the assembled dignitaries the "real reason" why he wrote in Yiddish. He explained that he liked to write ghost stories and that nothing suited a ghost better than a language that was dead, or at least dying. Then he went on to repeat the ten reasons why he liked to write for children that he had first enumerated at the National Book Award presentation in 1970.

Although Isaac's energies were severely tested by the nonstop activities of the Nobel Prize–giving week in Sweden, his humor never seemed to fail him. When asked what he was going to do with the $165,000 prize money, he quipped that he was going to buy himself a new Yiddish typewriter because his old one had turned into a critic. It refused to work properly when it didn't like what he was writing!

A few years after he had received the Nobel Prize, Isaac tried to playfully dismiss this achievement by telling an interviewer, "When I was a boy they called me a liar . . . for telling stories. Now they call me a writer. It's more advanced, but it's the same thing."

What Isaac might have added is that all storytellers

Isaac received the Nobel Prize for Literature on
the stage of the Stockholm Concert Hall.

tell lies. It's how well they tell them—how imaginatively and how convincingly—that makes them good writers. And among the outstanding storytellers of his day, Isaac Bashevis Singer was one of the best.

7

Not an Ending

A few years after Isaac had received the Nobel Prize, author and critic Herbert Mitgang asked him, "When do you do your writing?" Isaac calmly and uncomplainingly replied, "Between telephone calls."

It was indeed true that after becoming a Nobel laureate, Isaac continued to be just as generous as before in filling requests for appearances and interviews. He lectured extensively, met frequently with reporters, and even went so far as to interview himself!

The occasion for this interview was the 1983 release of the movie version of Isaac's short story "Yentl the Yeshiva Boy," which he had written in the 1950s. Since the 1970s, a number of Isaac's works had been made into plays, recordings, and film strips, and his novel

The Magician of Lublin was turned into a Hollywood film—although not very successfully—in 1979.

"Yentl," however, had already appeared as a highly praised stage presentation in 1974, so hopes were high for the movie. It was written, directed, and produced by Barbra Streisand, who also appeared in the leading role as Yentl.

But Isaac, who could be just as sharp and critical as he could be gentle and humorous, didn't like the movie version at all. And he didn't hesitate to say so in his "interview with himself," which appeared in *The New York Times* on January 29, 1984.

Among his questions, Isaac asked himself whether he liked the singing in this musical film version of the story. He replied that he had "never imagined Yentl singing songs," songs that were in no way related to *his* Yentl's "passion for learning." He was especially disturbed by the movie's ending, in which Yentl goes "on a ship to America, singing at the top of her lungs."

"Why," Isaac wondered, "would she decide to go to America?" There were still plenty of yeshivas in Poland where the devout Yentl could have continued to study after fleeing Avigdor, the male yeshiva student to whom she had become attracted.

Although many people enjoyed the movie for the type of entertainment it was, Isaac felt that it departed too drastically from his story *and* from the screenplay he had written for the film, which had been rejected. Perhaps, Isaac concluded, all really good plays were best written *as* plays. The successful transformation of a story or novel into a stage production or screenplay had to be done by a master. To do a good job, Isaac jested, was almost as impossible as trying "to make from a borscht a chicken soup."

More in keeping with its source material was the 1989 movie *Enemies, A Love Story*. This film was adapted from the novel of the same name, which Isaac had first written in 1966 and which had been published in English in 1972. Directed and produced by Paul Mazursky, the film dealt with the haunted lives of four Holocaust survivors—a man and three women—attempting to work out their troubled relationships in New York City in 1949.

In 1987, when Isaac was eighty-three, he and Alma decided to make their home year-round in Florida. The New York winters and the need to travel back and forth between their two residences were becoming a strain on Isaac's declining health. Nonetheless, Isaac continued to publish novels, short-story collections, and children's books.

Not all of the works that appeared during the 1980s were newly written. Some had been published earlier in a slightly different form, as was Isaac's 1982 novel for children *The Golem*. This story, out of Jewish folklore, had first appeared in Yiddish in *The Jewish Daily Forward* in 1969. Yet, like so much of Isaac's writing, it was such good storytelling that it could be enjoyed equally by children and adults.

A golem was a sort of Frankenstein's monster that could be made to serve the Jewish people in a time of trouble. It was a gigantic male figure made of clay that could be brought to life only when one of the holy names of God was inscribed on its forehead. In Isaac's

Alma and Isaac made their home year-round in Florida.

story, Rabbi Leib, a great scholar and mystic of the city of Prague, creates a golem that saves a pious Jew from being sentenced to death through the accusations of a wicked count.

God's command is that the golem must be destroyed after it has worked its miracle. But greedy for more miracles, the rabbi foolishly allows the golem to live. Soon it turns into an uncontrollable and destructive monster that terrorizes the entire city. It is only through the golem's all-too-human love for a serving maid that the rabbi is finally able to subdue it. The holy name is erased from the golem's forehead, and the creature once more becomes a lifeless lump of clay.

Isaac's last book for children was published in 1984. Titled *Stories for Children*, it was a collection of some of his very best short stories—scary ones and tender ones, family stories about the celebration of Jewish holidays, and funny stories about the fools of Chelm and other shlemiels of this world.

In an introductory note, Isaac described how he had been encouraged to start writing for children by Elizabeth Shub, a friend of many years. The two met for the first time in 1935, soon after Isaac arrived in America. Elizabeth Shub, then in her teens, was the daughter of a prominent writer for the Yiddish-language newspaper, the *Day*.

Later she became an editor and translator of some of Isaac's works. Deeply impressed by his storytelling skills, she suggested he write something for young readers. In the 1960s, in response to her urging, Isaac wrote his first story for children, "Zlateh the Goat."

During the latter half of the 1980s, as Isaac approached his final years, some of his work for adult readers began to show traces of dismay and even despair. The questions that had troubled Isaac from childhood had still not been resolved for him. He believed in God, but God's silence and lack of mercy bothered him.

Isaac in his final years.

Why did so much evil and injustice continue to exist in the world?

Isaac was above all truthful. Often the endings of his own stories were vague and unsatisfying, for he knew that there were no easy answers. Perhaps it was this knowledge—his sense that the struggle between good and evil would continue until the end of time—that seemed to have saddened him toward the end of his own existence.

On July 24, 1991, at the age of eighty-seven, Isaac Bashevis Singer died in Florida, after a series of strokes. His body was flown to New York, where a funeral service took place on Sunday, July 28, in the upper Manhattan neighborhood that had long been his home. Although Isaac had left the area four years earlier, he was still warmly remembered by neighbors and friends, and especially by the waiters in his favorite dairy restaurants and other eateries.

The upper Broadway scene, once heavily populated by refugees from Hitler's Europe, had been changing gradually. But it was still haunted by ghosts, not unlike those in Isaac's story "The Cafeteria," which had appeared in his 1970 collection *A Friend of Kafka and Other Stories*. In the story, Esther, a Holocaust survivor, unable to sleep, visits a neighborhood cafeteria in the small hours of the morning, assuming that it remains open all night. Although the window is covered by a curtain, the revolving door turns and she enters. Inside she witnesses a horrifying sight. The tables have been pushed together and at the head stands Adolf Hitler, haranguing a large gathering of Nazis. One of them turns to look at her and she runs out, trembling.

The next morning, she learns that the cafeteria has burned to the ground. Did Esther really see Hitler and his followers, or were the demons of the past playing tricks on her?

Visitors from the spirit world may also have been hovering about at Isaac's funeral service. When an unexplained growling issued from the chapel's amplifier system during the rabbi's eulogy, the rabbi himself suggested, "Those are demons." In the midst of their grief, the mourners smiled, certain that Isaac would have been rather pleased to think that some of his imps and goblins were playfully making their presence known.

Principal among the mourners were Isaac's wife of fifty-one years, Alma, and his son, Israel Zamir, who had flown in from Israel. Others included Isaac's publishers, translators, illustrators, fellow writers, and numerous friends and admirers. Isaac had often voiced his thoughts about death, both in his writing and in talks with interviewers, and these thoughts were somehow comforting in a time of sadness.

In the closing lines of his novel *The Family Moskat*, Isaac had written, "Death is the Messiah." And in an interview with Richard Burgin, he repeated his belief that death is the only true redemption, for "the promise which death gives to people is always kept."

Isaac was also often asked if he believed in an afterlife. His response reflected the faith to which he'd always clung. "The human spirit," he insisted, "does not end with physical death . . . every soul who ever lived is here in one way or another."

The death of Isaac Bashevis Singer was most certainly not an ending, for his legacy was an incredibly rich one. As a last link with the world of Eastern European Jewry, he drew us an indelible picture of a vanished past and gave a dying language an extended life. His magic made the world of the supernatural real to us, and he even managed to tickle our funny bones. Best of all, he knew how to tell us a story.

IMPORTANT DATES

1904   Isaac Bashevis Singer is born Icek-Hersz Zynger in Leoncin, Poland. July 14 will be observed as his birthday, although he was probably born in the fall of that year.

1907   Isaac's family moves to Radzymin, Poland.

1908   The Singers make their home at Number 10 Krochmalna Street, in the Polish capital of Warsaw, where they remain until 1914.

1914   The family moves to Number 12 Krochmalna Street.

1917   Isaac becomes bar mitzvah. Soon afterward, he leaves Warsaw for Bilgoray, his mother's birthplace in southern Poland.

1921   Isaac enrolls in the Tachkemoni Rabbinical Seminary in Warsaw. After about a year, he returns to Bilgoray.

1922   Isaac joins his parents in the southern Polish town of Dzikow.

1923   At the invitation of his older brother, Israel Joshua,

Isaac returns to Warsaw to work as a proofreader for a Yiddish literary magazine.

1927   Isaac's first published short story, "In Old Age," appears in the magazine *Literary Pages*.

1934   Isaac's first novel, *Satan in Goray*, appears in installments in the Yiddish-language Polish magazine *Globus*.

1935   Isaac leaves Poland for the United States to begin writing free-lance material for *The Jewish Daily Forward*.

1940   Isaac marries Alma Haimann Wasserman, a German-Jewish refugee.

1943   Isaac becomes an American citizen.

1944   Israel Joshua, Isaac's older brother who has established a distinguished literary reputation, dies.

1945   Isaac's second novel, *The Family Moskat*, begins to appear in serialized form in the *Forward*.

1953   The short story "Gimpel the Fool" is published in an American magazine in English translation and brings Isaac wider recognition.

1955   *Satan in Goray* is published in English in book form.

1957   *Gimpel the Fool and Other Stories* is published in English in book form, the first of many short-story collections.

1964   Isaac is elected to the National Institute of Arts and Letters, its only American member who writes in a language other than English.

1966   *Zlateh the Goat and Other Stories*, Isaac's first book for children, wins him his first Newbery Honor Book Award. Also, his first memoir, *In My Father's Court*, is published in English.

1970   *A Day of Pleasure: Stories of a Boy Growing Up in Warsaw* wins the National Book Award for children's literature, and Isaac gives ten of the five hundred reasons why he writes for children.

1978　The Nobel Prize for Literature is awarded to Isaac Bashevis Singer. In his Nobel lecture, Isaac includes words in Yiddish expressing his gratitude for the high honor bestowed upon him and the Yiddish language.

1983　The short story "Yentl the Yeshiva Boy" appears as a major Hollywood movie.

1989　The movie version of the novel *Enemies, A Love Story* is released to critical acclaim.

1991　On July 24, Isaac Bashevis Singer dies in Florida. His funeral, held in New York City, is attended by his numerous friends, colleagues, and admirers.

BIBLIOGRAPHY

Alexander, Edward. *Isaac Bashevis Singer*. Boston: Twayne Publishers, 1980.

Allentuck, Marcia, editor. *The Achievement of Isaac Bashevis Singer*. Carbondale and Edwardsville, Ill.: Southern Illinois University Press, 1969.

Buchen, Irving H. *Isaac Bashevis Singer and the Eternal Past*. New York: New York University Press, 1968.

Epstein, Joseph. "Our Debt to I. B. Singer." *Commentary*, November 1991.

Evory, Ann, editor. *Contemporary Authors: New Revision Series, Volume I*. Detroit: Gale Research Company, 1981.

Hurwitz, Johanna. "I. B. Singer: He's a Story in Himself." *Newsday*, October 15, 1978.

Kresh, Paul. *Isaac Bashevis Singer: The Magician of West 86th Street*. New York: The Dial Press, 1979.

Kresh, Paul. *Isaac Bashevis Singer: The Story of a Storyteller*.* New York: Lodestar Books, E. P. Dutton, 1984.

*Juvenile title

Malin, Irving. *Isaac Bashevis Singer*. New York: Frederick Unger Publishing Company, 1972.

Mitgang, Herbert. "There Is a Power That Takes Care of Writers." *The New York Times Book Review*, June 30, 1985.

Shenker, Israel. "The Man Who Talked Back to God: Isaac Bashevis Singer, 1904–1991." *The New York Times Book Review*, August 11, 1991.

Sinclair, Clive. *The Brothers Singer*. London: Allison and Busby, Ltd., 1983.

Singer, Isaac Bashevis. "I. B. Singer Talks to I. B. Singer About the Movie 'Yentl.' " *The New York Times*, January 29, 1984.

Singer, Isaac Bashevis, and Richard Burgin. *Conversations with Isaac Bashevis Singer*. New York: Doubleday and Company, 1985.

Singer, Isaac Bashevis, and Richard Burgin. "Isaac Bashevis Singer Talks . . . About Everything." *The New York Times Magazine*, November 26, 1978.

Singer, Isaac Bashevis, and Richard Burgin. "Isaac Bashevis Singer's Universe." *The New York Times Magazine*, December 3, 1978.

Singer, I. J. *Of a World That Is No More*. New York: Vanguard Press, 1970.

Wasson, Tyler, editor. *Nobel Prize Winners*. New York: The H. W. Wilson Company, 1987.

WORKS BY
ISAAC BASHEVIS SINGER

(in order of their publication
in book form in English)

Novels

The Family Moskat. New York: Alfred A. Knopf, 1950.
Satan in Goray. New York: Noonday Press, 1955.
The Magician of Lublin. New York: Noonday Press, 1960.
The Slave. New York: Farrar, Straus and Cudahy, 1962.
The Manor. New York: Farrar, Straus and Giroux, 1967.
The Estate. New York: Farrar, Straus and Giroux, 1969.
Enemies, A Love Story. New York: Farrar, Straus and Giroux, 1972.
Shosha. New York: Farrar, Straus and Giroux, 1978.
The Reaches of Heaven: A Story of the Baal Shem Tov. New York: Farrar, Straus and Giroux, 1980.
The Penitent. New York: Farrar, Straus and Giroux, 1983.
The King of the Fields. New York: Farrar, Straus and Giroux, 1988.
Scum. New York: Farrar, Straus and Giroux, 1991.
The Certificate. New York: Farrar, Straus and Giroux, 1992.
Meshugah. New York: Farrar, Straus and Giroux, 1994.

Short Story Collections

Gimpel the Fool and Other Stories. New York: Noonday Press, 1957.

The Spinoza of Market Street and Other Stories. New York: Farrar, Straus and Cudahy, 1961.

Short Friday and Other Stories. New York: Farrar, Straus and Giroux, 1964.

Selected Short Stories of Isaac Bashevis Singer. New York: The Modern Library, 1966.

The Séance and Other Stories. New York: Farrar, Straus and Giroux, 1968.

A Friend of Kafka and Other Stories. New York: Farrar, Straus and Giroux, 1970.

An Isaac Bashevis Singer Reader. New York: Farrar, Straus and Giroux, 1971.

A Crown of Feathers and Other Stories. New York: Farrar, Straus and Giroux, 1973.

Passions and Other Stories. New York: Farrar, Straus and Giroux, 1975.

Old Love and Other Stories. New York: Farrar, Straus and Giroux, 1979.

The Collected Stories of Isaac Bashevis Singer. New York: Farrar, Straus and Giroux, 1982.

The Image and Other Stories. New York: Farrar, Straus and Giroux, 1985.

The Death of Methuselah and Other Stories. New York: Farrar, Straus and Giroux, 1988.

Memoirs

In My Father's Court. New York: Farrar, Straus and Giroux, 1966.

A Little Boy in Search of God. Garden City, N.Y.: Doubleday, 1976.

A Young Man in Search of Love. Garden City, N.Y.: Doubleday, 1978.

Lost in America. Garden City, N.Y.: Doubleday, 1979.

Children's Books

Zlateh the Goat and Other Stories. New York: Harper & Row, 1966.

The Fearsome Inn. New York: Scribner's, 1967.

Mazel and Shlimazel; or, The Milk of a Lioness. New York: Farrar, Straus and Giroux, 1967.

When Shlemiel Went to Warsaw and Other Stories. New York: Farrar, Straus and Giroux, 1968.

A Day of Pleasure: Stories of a Boy Growing Up in Warsaw. New York: Farrar, Straus and Giroux, 1969.

Elijah the Slave. New York: Farrar, Straus and Giroux, 1970.

Joseph and Koza; or, The Sacrifice to the Vistula. New York: Farrar, Straus and Giroux, 1970.

Alone in the Wild Forest. New York: Farrar, Straus and Giroux, 1971.

The Topsy-Turvy Emperor of China. New York: Harper & Row, 1971.

The Wicked City. New York: Farrar, Straus and Giroux, 1972.

The Fools of Chelm and Their History. New York: Farrar, Straus and Giroux, 1973.

Why Noah Chose the Dove. New York: Farrar, Straus and Giroux, 1974.

A Tale of Three Wishes. New York: Farrar, Straus and Giroux, 1976.

Naftali the Storyteller and His Horse, Sus, and Other Stories. New York: Farrar, Straus and Giroux, 1976.

The Power of Light: Eight Stories for Hanukkah. New York: Farrar, Straus and Giroux, 1980.

The Golem. New York: Farrar, Straus and Giroux, 1982.

Stories for Children. New York: Farrar, Straus and Giroux, 1984.

INDEX